Tongues on Fire

The Fallacy of Tongues as a Language of Prayer

R.L. Pich

ISBN 979-8-89428-291-6 (paperback)
ISBN 979-8-89428-292-3 (digital)

Christian Faith Publishing
832 Park Avenue
Meadville, PA 16335
www.christianfaithpublishing.com

Printed in the United States of America

Introduction

It has been over two thousand years, and the debate still flourishes among Christian denominations regarding what the Bible teaches about speaking and praying in tongues. The answer to that question and how spiritual gifts, in general, are manifested is as varied as the groups that make up the organized church. By far, the groups that have placed the greatest emphasis on the manifestation of spiritual gifts, in particular speaking in tongues, are the modern Pentecostal and charismatic movements. Pentecostals have their own denominations and churches, whereas charismatics can be found in most denominations. For this book, the name Pentecostals will be used to include both movements. Although there are some differences among these two groups, there is little to distinguish one from the other regarding the gift of tongues. Both believe that all spiritual gifts, including tongues, are operational today.

The operation of the tongues gift by Pentecostals is, without argument, the defining element of their group. It is such a fundamental requirement within the movement that they not only pressure those within the group to speak in tongues,[1] but they also begin teaching how to speak in tongues as early as kindergarten in their Sunday school curriculums. It is viewed by Pentecostals as the test of the Holy Spirit's presence in the life of the believer, and without it, they teach that a major spiritual dimension is lacking in that individual. Evidence of this can be seen in the following children's Sunday school lesson, "The common New Testament experience of those baptized in the Holy Spirit was speaking with other tongues. This prayer language is given as a sign that you have received the gift. The Biblical record shows in Acts that believers received power and a prayer language when baptized in the Holy Spirit."[2]

This teaching has made its way into other Christian groups as well. In a recent study, almost half of Southern Baptist Convention (SBC) pastors, a Christian group considered one of the most conservative of denominations, believe speaking in tongues is a gift that all believers can experience. Recently, SBC relaxed its traditional position of restricting its use to allow for new missionary candidates to hold the Pentecostal view of tongues and still qualify for positions within the SBC.[3] It is not just SBC leadership that has embraced this teaching, but in a recent Sunday School class in a Southern Baptist church, the question was asked how many have prayed in tongues. Over half the class raised their hands in the affirmative.[4]

If indeed the modern tongues movement is an error, there are worse things than speaking in tongues a believer can participate in, and many would argue that speaking and praying in tongues is one of the most spiritually uplifting benefits of the indwelling Holy Spirit. The debate only highlights the importance for believers to search the scriptures and test whether the Pentecostal view is sound doctrine or false teaching. Rather than avoiding the issue for the sake of unity, every believer should be concerned about the truth of any teaching that deviates from the written word. (1 Thessalonians 5:21, 1 Timothy 1:10, 2 Tim 4:3, Titus 1:9, Titus 2:1, Jude 3)

Chapter 1

Will the Real Tongues Please Stand Up

The gift of tongues is indeed listed as one of the manifestations of the Holy Spirit given to believers. It is mentioned in five places in the New Testament: Mark 16, Acts 2, Acts 10, Acts 19, and 1 Corinthians, where Paul devotes the entire fourteenth chapter of 1 Corinthians to regulate its use in the Church. In fact, the gift of tongues is the only spiritual gift that comes with restrictions regarding its use. The Church in Corinth had perverted the use of tongues as God had intended, and Paul was writing to this carnal and immature church to correct their misuse of this spiritual gift.[5]

The gift of tongues is first listed in the New Testament in Mark 16:17–18, where it is identified as one of the signs that would follow those who believed. The other signs are healing, casting out devils, drinking something deadly and not being hurt, and taking up deadly serpents without harm. It is interesting to note that Pentecostals use these verses in Mark 16 to validate their practice of speaking in tongues, exorcism, and healing gifts for the present. It is curious that they fail to mention the other two, drinking something deadly and taking up deadly serpents, as being operational today as well. Perhaps that is because some of the signs listed in Mark 16 are easier to falsify, whereas drinking poison and handling deadly serpents would incur quite a bit more risk and would be more difficult to imitate, as the Appalachian snake handler cult can attest.[6] No one has adequately explained why the Pentecostals emphasize tongues and healing for the present and exclude the other signs listed in Mark 16.

A legitimate question is raised regarding the instruction of Mark 16 regarding the permanence of the gift of tongues. Jesus said these five signs would follow those who believe; tongues, healing, exorcism, and not being hurt by poison or deadly snakes. If tongues and the other signs were not for today, then why would Jesus say that they would follow those who believe, indicating their continued operation? For those who believe tongues are not a gift for today, the scriptural explanation would be that in the crowd Jesus was speaking to, there were some who didn't believe. Matthew 28:16–17 says, "Then the eleven disciples went away into Galilee, into a mountain where Jesus had appointed them. And when they saw him, they worshipped him: but some doubted." It doesn't say who it was that doubted or if it was one of the eleven apostles or, more probably, one of the other disciples of Jesus. It is remarkable that even after the resurrection and multiple appearances to his disciples, some still doubted it. He would not have been speaking to those who doubted but to those in the crowd who believed.

The coming of the Holy Spirit in Acts 2 was a unique event in the history of the church. It was the day the church was born and the fulfillment of the promised indwelling of believers. When the Holy Spirit came upon the disciples in the upper room, along with speaking in tongues there were cloves of fire descending upon each one and the sound of a rushing wind so cacophonous that the entire city came to investigate. If there was nothing unique about the Acts 2 experience, and Pentecost can be experienced by every believer, then it is reasonable to expect the other manifestations of the Holy Spirit to continue as well. There would be no reason to assume otherwise. Fire and wind were as much a part of the Holy Spirit's indwelling on the day of Pentecost as speaking in tongues. Excluding fire and wind would certainly appear to be inconsistent with the Pentecostal view that what was promised in Mark 16 and what occurred in Acts 2 should be the expectation of all believers. As we shall discuss later, these five signs listed in Mark 16 were called signs, not gifts. Signs were given to the apostles and those with them to validate the message of the gospel in miraculous ways (Mark 16:20, Acts 2:43, 5:12, 14:3; Rom 15:19; 2 Cor 12:12) and were not given as permanent gifts for the church (Hebrew 2:4).

Tongues are mentioned in the Bible as far back as Isaiah, where the prophet foretold the coming of a sign for the people of Israel, "For with stammering lips and another tongue He will speak to these people, to whom He said, this is the rest with which you may cause the weary to rest, and, this is refreshing, yet they would not hear. But the word of the LORD was to them, precept upon precept, precept upon precept, line upon line, line upon line, here a little, there a little, that they might go and fall backward, and be broken and snared and caught" Isaiah 28:11–13. Isaiah was a pronouncing judgment upon the people of Israel because of their rejection of God, and in the future, the message of God's salvation, which the nation would reject, would come from a Gentile tongue, not from the Hebrew tongue. This would have been completely unacceptable to the Jewish people to think that God would speak through any people other than the Jews. And yet, God foretold that the sign of tongues would signify the new and better way, that salvation would come through the Messiah Jesus Christ, and it would be proclaimed through other tongues.

There is a principle of interpretation called the principle of first mention, which states that whenever a doctrine is first mentioned in the Bible, that occurrence generally defines the doctrine for subsequent understanding.[7] This certainly holds true for the doctrine of tongues as well. The apostle Paul confirms the sign aspect of tongues in 1 Corinthians 14: 21–22 when he writes," In the law, it is written: with men of other tongues and other lips I will speak to this people; And yet, for all that, they will not hear Me, says the Lord. Therefore, tongues are for a sign, not to those who believe but to unbelievers; but prophesying is not for unbelievers but for those who believe."

The New Testament word for tongues is the Greek word "glossa," which means languages. Both the prophet Isaiah and the apostle Paul confirmed that the primary purpose of the gift of tongues was to be a sign given to confirm the message of the apostles and those with them in the furtherance of the gospel during the transition period when God first opened salvation by grace through faith to all who would believe in the atonement of Christ. We see this clearly exhibited in Acts chapter 2, where Peter confirmed the working of God and the message of the risen Christ to the Jews who had gathered and were perplexed at the speaking of the various languages by the disciples whom they considered ignorant inebriated hicks from Galilee.

The second event where tongues were present was in Acts chapter 10, the outpouring of salvation upon the Gentiles. God confirmed to Peter the door of salvation was opened to the Gentiles by the sign of Cornelius and his household speaking in tongues. The fact that this was an extraordinary event is evidenced by Peter's astonishment at the manifestation of tongues at the conversion of this Gentile and his household (Acts 10:45). His reaction is telling when Peter reports to the Jewish believers about this extraordinary event, "And as I began to speak, the Holy Spirit fell upon them, as upon us at the beginning" (Acts 11:15). The phrase "at the beginning" would indicate Peter's understanding that this manifestation of the Holy Spirit in tongues was not a recurring event with every conversion but was as unique an event as was the first coming of the Spirit at Pentecost.

Again, in Acts chapter 19, God confirms the superior message of the gospel of Christ over the message of John the Baptist by the filling of the twelve Ephesian disciples of John with His Holy Spirit and the confirming presence of the gift of tongues. In a real sense, these Ephesian disciples of John the Baptist were Old Testament believers waiting for the promised coming of the Messiah. God was confirming that Jesus is indeed the Christ, the Son of the living God, and not just an add-on to previous Old Testament beliefs no matter how godly the believers or how sincere their faith, but an entirely new and better way. Both the experiences of Acts 10 and Acts 19 illustrate the sign aspect of this gift. God used extraordinary signs to confirm extraordinary facts.

It should be noted that in all the other instances of conversion given in the book of Acts other than in chapters two, ten, and nineteen, speaking in tongues is not mentioned. The assumption by Pentecostals is that they were indeed present, just not mentioned. Should we then assume that the other so-called manifestations of the Spirit promulgated by Pentecostals, such as being slain in the Spirit, being drunk in the Spirit, and frenzied shaking of the body by the Spirit, were also present, though not mentioned? Should we assume that flaming tongues of fire and the sound of hurricane-force winds were present as well with each new conversion? Not even Pentecostals would concur with that possibility. There is no reason to believe that tongues were present but not mentioned except to validate a predetermined belief.

Although not specifically mentioned in scripture, there is the possibility that the gift of languages was given to individuals by the sovereign will of God for the purpose of communicating the gospel as it spread to the uttermost parts of the world. That could be the basis of Paul's statement that he spoke in tongues more than anyone. As an apostle to the gentiles, it would have been a useful tool as he moved through the areas of Asia Minor preaching the salvation message. Although we can't be dogmatic about that, it would not be an unreasonable assumption. Even if that were the case, it would not preclude the use of tongues as a sign and not as a permanent gift to the church.

To assume that Paul prayed in tongues more than anyone at Corinth (1 Corinthians 14:18), as some Pentecostal writers suggest, is not an assumption supported by the scriptures. Paul uses both speaking and praying in tongues in his discussion regarding the use of this gift and it is not reasonable to conclude he would have been confused as to which of those he was referring to. If he meant that he prayed in tongues more than anyone, he certainly could have said so. It is an important distinction because Paul never talks about personally praying in tongues, and nowhere in scripture does it indicate that anyone else prayed in tongues outside of Corinth. As far as we know from scripture, praying in tongues was only a phenomenon in the church in Corinth, and Paul was writing to correct the Corinthians in their exercise of this sign gift. Paul never addresses this issue in any of his other epistles. While the sign gift of tongues was obviously functioning in the Corinthian church as demonstrated by Paul's exhortations regarding its use, it is apparent by his instruction to the church that the spiritual gift of tongues had become corrupted, devolving into a selfish spectacle.

Chapter 2

Going, Going, Gone

Speaking in tongues is not a recent phenomenon in the church. After the apostolic age, there are isolated instances of this practice addressed by church leaders throughout church history, primarily regarding heresies and aberrant practices of cult leaders. An important heresy the church addressed was Montanism, which became popular in the late second century AD. This movement was started by Montanus, who stressed the importance of speaking in tongues, prophecy, and miraculous gifts. He taught that the prophetic power of the Holy Spirit took residence in him and whomever he passed that power onto by the laying on of hands. This is a common practice among Pentecostals today. He claimed that this special residence of the Holy Spirit was not given to everyone but to him and to whom he chose to endow. He empowered female followers he called his prophetesses, enabling them to speak revelation which had the equivalent authority of scripture.

Montanus claimed he had the gift of prophecy and that the Holy Spirit spoke directly through him, a belief widely dismissed by early church leaders except Tertullian and a few others. One early church writer, Hippolytus, wrote, "They are beguiled by two females whom they consider prophetesses…They pretend that these see certain things by means of the Paraclete in them. They implicitly believe what these utter, and give out that they learnt more from their revelations than from the law, the prophets, and the gospels". Concerning the speaking in tongues by Montanus, another writer wrote, "So then he was carried away by the spirit and wrought up into a certain kind of frenzy and irregular ecstasy, raving and speaking and uttering strange things and proclaiming what was contrary to the institutions that had prevailed in the church. He excited two other females and filled them with the spirit of delusion so that they also speak like the former in a kind of ecstasy and out of season, and in a manner strange and novel."[8]

We should be mindful of how the early church dealt with this issue. The doctrines of the church were new, not having been revealed in the Old Testament (Ephesians 3). The early church had to struggle with understanding and defining these doctrines for perpetuity. They struggled mightily to understand and honor the truth revealed in the word now completed. If tongues were a standard expectation after conversion, as Pentecostal writers claim, then it would not have seemed bizarre and strange when it was encountered by the early church. It would have been no more unusual than the expectation to meet, pray, or study the word. Conversion, receiving the Holy Spirit, speaking, and praying in tongues would have been a frequent occurrence, even a mundane one. But it wasn't. It seemed strange and suspicious to them, and leaders like Montanus and his teachings were called into question.

Some might argue that the doctrine of tongues was treated by the early church much like salvation by grace through faith was treated later in church history. Salvation by grace was a truth suppressed by the Papal church until

Martin Luther reclaimed it during the Reformation. Perhaps tongues suffered the same repression under the weight of the organized church. But during the second and third centuries, the doctrine of the Holy Spirit was not lost. This was the epoch of the persecuted church, the age of completion of the New Testament, and the defining of the doctrines of the church. There was no organized repression of the truth but a robust quest to define and champion it.

After the fourth century, Montanus's teachings and the infrequent appearance of tongues by other groups were deemed heretical and rejected. This was the position of the church and remained so until the seventeenth century when tongues resurfaced in vigor to the church that had become stagnant and ritualistic, lacking in true spiritual depth. People hungered for a deeper spiritual experience and were often led astray by the emotional appeal of this new Pentecost experience. The Quakers, the Shakers, and the "holy rollers" offered a more exciting and fulfilling, albeit erroneous, path to spiritual enlightenment, and many followed.

In practice, there is very little difference between the modern tongues movement and the heresies of the past. The claim of a privileged reception of special Holy Spirit powers, the passing of the spirit to others by the laying on of hands, speaking in tongues, frenzied convulsive behavior, uncontrolled states of trance and ecstasy, miraculous manifestations of supernatural power, and prophetic utterances common among Pentecostal revival meetings of today were carefully examined in the past by the early church fathers and found to be in error. Scrutiny reveals the same can be said of the current claims of Pentecostal groups as well.

The modern expansion of tongues-speaking and other supposed manifestations attributed to the Holy Spirit can be traced back to its reintroduction into mainstream

Christianity primarily through mass media. When cable television began making entrance into homes across the globe, one station became a showcase for Pentecostal programming. GodTV is a United Kingdom TV programming ministry founded in 1995 by Rory and Wendy Alec, whose mission, they state, is to discover and promote ministries where the Holy Spirit is working, and lives are being changed. GodTV saw spectacular growth, and its impact can't be overstated. GodTV programming is varied but leans heavily toward the Pentecostal viewpoint. According to GodTV's founder, Rory Alec, GodTV has "searched through the earth for those events and anointings that the Lord has laid on our hearts to amplify their message and anointing for the body of Christ in this crucial end-time hour that we live in."[9] As Wendy Alec, director of programming for GodTV stated, "For the first time in history, revival is literally being ignited across the airwaves."[10]

One revivalist personality showcased on GodTV was Todd Bentley, a self-proclaimed, heavily tattooed, and body-pierced prophet who conducted nightly healing and prophetic meetings in Lakeland, Florida. His gatherings regularly drew thousands of attendees, with a potential TV audience on GodTV of over 850 million viewers. His "Lakeland Outpouring" was a nightly broadcast on GodTV featuring supposed healings and other spectacular supernatural events until Bently's extramarital affair and divorce made headlines. Through this and other like programs, what had been percolating in fringe Christian Pentecostal groups was introduced to mainstream Christianity, perhaps too many for the first.

The emphasis on speaking in tongues, healings, mystic manifestations, and prophetic declarations became a common feature of these televised revival meetings. But along with these, more bizarre elements were also introduced to the viewers, such as violent shaking of the head and body, being "slain" in the spirit where a person loses consciousness and lapses into trancelike states, being "drunk in the Spirit" as if intoxicated, frenzied running, leaping, and jumping through the arena, barking and screeching like animals, and even claims of the dead being raised and limbs being regrown to name a few. Although the Todd Bentley revivals claimed a vast number of healings and miracles, no proof of any of the claimed miracles was ever produced when requested by an ABC Nightline investigation into the validity of Bently's revival. Shortly after the Nightline program critical of Bently's claims aired, Bently suspended his Lakeland revival.[11] In 2020, *Christianity Today* declared Bently unfit for ministry due to credible allegations of adultery, sexting, and substance abuse spanning the previous fifteen years.[12]

The Pentecostal programming of GodTV was part of an explosion of similar high profile, high visibility ministries gaining popularity, such as the Toronto Outpouring, The Kansas City prophets, the International House of Prayer, Ben Johnson and Bethel church in California, and various other Televangelist ministries which celebrated charismatic elements and activities of Pentecostal theology. These and others like them helped propel Pentecostal teaching into mainstream Christianity.

Many of these ministries promote what was known as the "Latter Rain Movement" based on Joel 2: 28–29, "And it shall come to pass afterward that I will pour out My Spirit on all flesh; Your sons and your daughters shall prophesy, Your old men shall dream dreams, Your young men shall see visions. And also on My menservants and on My maidservants I will pour out My Spirit in those days," and a cryptic understanding of Joel 2:23, "Be glad then, you children of Zion, and rejoice in the LORD your God; for He has given you the former rain faithfully, and He will cause the rain to come down for you—the former rain, and the latter rain in the first month." Proponents of this view teach that the latter rain spoken of by Joel 2:28–29 is a promise of a supernatural and unprecedented outpouring of the Holy Spirit on the church to come prior to Christ's return.

Visions, miracles, supernatural cosmic occurrences, angelic visitations, transport to heaven to speak personally with Jesus, speaking in tongues, healings, and other phenomena are all supposed manifestations of this "latter rain" Holy Spirit outpouring. Modern movements such as the Brownsville/Pensacola Revival, the Toronto Blessing, and the "holy laughter" phenomenon contain principles of Latter Rain theology.[13] This anticipated end times outpouring of the Holy Spirit and the accompanying signs and wonders can be found in much of the Pentecostal writing, as evidenced by this quote from Dave Robertson in his book on praying in tongues, "He (God) was saying that the time had come to share in a broader measure the revelation knowledge He had given me over the years regarding praying in tongues. The message had come to maturity for the body of Christ."

This is a deceptive enticement that draws immature believers into the belief that God is doing something today in the church that He has not done in the past. It is alluring to think that one might be missing out on some new thing God is doing. Those believers in the past could not experience it, but we can experience it as the age draws to a close. This belief has no basis in biblical teaching. What the Bible does teach is that evil men will grow worse and that there will be a proliferation of deceptive signs and wonders, culminating in the appearance of Antichrist. We are to be vigilant in the last days, guarding against deceivers, false teachers, and satanic signs and wonders (Matthew 24:24, 2 Peter 2:1).

Until recent church history, it was generally accepted that the gift of tongues ended at the end of the first century after the completion of the New Testament. None of the epistles after Corinthians mention tongues, and the extensive writings of the early church leaders questioned its use. Apart from sporadic occurrences, It seemed to have ceased until its reemergence in the seventeenth century and promulgated in earnest in the eighteenth century up to today.[14] This early disappearance of tongues is consistent with the New Testament writings of Paul in 1 Corinthians 13:8, where Paul says, "Love never fails. But whether there are prophecies, they will fail; whether there are tongues, they will cease; whether there is knowledge, it will vanish away." A careful examination of this verse shows three gifts are mentioned: tongues, prophecy, and knowledge, and all three are said to eventually come to an end.

In 1 Cor 13:9–10, both prophecy and knowledge are said to end when that which is perfect comes, "For we know in part, and we prophesy in part. But when that which is perfect has come, then that which is in part will be done away." It is clear from this passage and 1 Corinthians 13:8 that all three gifts, knowledge, prophecy, and tongues, will come to an end. There are two views as to when the two gifts, prophecy, and knowledge, will end. The gift of prophecy is primarily the ability to proclaim God's revealed truth, and knowledge is the Spirit-led understanding of His word for the benefit of edifying the church. One view is that they will end at the perfect appearance of our Lord Jesus Christ and the coming of His kingdom. In the eternal state, there will no longer be a need for these two gifts as we will all know as we are known (1 Corinthians 13:12). The other view is that they ended when the perfect word of God, the New Testament, was completed and these revelatory gifts were no longer needed (James 1: 22–26.) In the completed word of God, we now have everything we need to do the will of God (Romans 12:2, 2 Corinthians 3:18). Regardless of which view is adopted, the salient point is that both the gifts of prophecy and knowledge will end when acted upon by an external cause.

However, tongues are said to end without any external cause or impetus. The verb "cease," used only in relation to tongues, is written in the middle voice in Greek, the language of the New Testament, which indicates that, unlike the other two, prophecy and knowledge, this gift will cease on its own.[15] Once Israel had solidified its rejection of their Messiah and the New Testament had been completed, the need for such a sign was no longer crucial, and it appears to have ceased. Although it may be true that a spiritual gift of languages was operational as the gospel message moved to new people groups, it is not specifically stated in the New Testament that such a gift is an ongoing reality, and nowhere in scripture does it teach that there is a continuing gift of unknown tongues to be used as a special Spirit prayer language as erroneously taught by Pentecostal groups today.[16]

Chapter 3

Type 1 And Type 2 Tongues

Pentecostal writers have attempted to separate the gift of tongues into multiple distinct categories. These distinctions include angelic languages, Holy Spirit created heavenly language, known and unknown tongues, and different kinds of tongues depending on whether they were being used for worship, interpretation, teaching, prophecy, or self-edification. Multiple verses of scripture are used to make these dissections.

An often-cited verse is found in 1 Corinthians 13:1, "Though I speak with the tongues of men and of angels, but have not love, I have become sounding brass or a clanging cymbal." Some Pentecostal apologists have suggested that what is being referenced in the verse above is the language of heaven spoken by angels and is, in fact, the same language as the prayer language of tongues, the term "tongues of men" referring to human languages and "tongues of angels" referring to a completely different and unknown angelic or heavenly language.[17]

The first category, called tongues of men, would be recognizable as the known human languages. The second category, called the tongues of angels, would be an entirely different kind of tongues, and their use would not be governed by the scriptural restrictions of 1 Corinthians 14. This second category, tongues of angels, is the secret spiritual prayer language of heaven available to all believers. Pentecostal writer Dave Robertson attempts to identify the tongues of angels as follows: "Tongues of angels is talking about the language used in heaven. I suspect that most of the time, we are speaking the language of angels when we pray in tongues to edify ourselves and to pray out the mysteries of God's plan for our lives."

In a different part of his book, he identifies the tongues prayer language as a unique fruit of the indwelling Spirit that is created in each believer word for word as the believer prays in the Spirit.[18] However, these two definitions of tongues appear to be mutually exclusive. Either the Spirit creates the unique prayer language for each believer word for word as they pray, or the tongues prayer language is a preexisting angelic language, but tongues can't be both since one is uniquely created and the other is a preexisting language. Certainly, no one would argue the absurdity that God creates the language for angels word for word as they speak. This type of inconsistency permeates Pentecostal theology as they seek to build their narrative on an erroneous foundation. It is another example of what one writer aptly calls the contorted chaos of charismatic confusion.

The Greek construct of 1 Corinthians 13:1 does not allow for the bifurcation promoted by the Pentecostal writers. The verse is not saying there is one type of tongue called the tongues of men and a completely unique and different kind of tongues, called the tongues of angels, one being uniquely human and the other being uniquely angelic. Verse 13:1 is constructed in Greek to indicate the word tongues is, in fact, modified by what follows, that is, by the human quality of one and the angelic quality of the other. The qualitative difference in the grammar of the verse would be like saying, "Though I speak with the tongues of third-grade educated Appalachian hillbillies or with the eloquence of Shakespearian trained thespians, if I don't have love, I am nothing." The emphasis is not on the different origins of the language but on the content and quality of the language.

This use of "tongue" to describe the eloquence of the language's content is further illustrated in the case of Moses as described in Exodus 4:10. "Then Moses said to the LORD, 'O my Lord, I *am* not eloquent, neither before nor since You have spoken to Your servant; but I *am* slow of speech and slow of tongue.'" Isaiah 50:4 further illustrates this quality of content when he writes: "The Lord GOD has given me the tongue of the learned, that I should know how to speak a word in season to him who is weary. He awakens me morning by morning; he awakens my ear to hear as learned."

Paul makes clear in 1 Corinthians 13:2 that it is not the origin of the language itself he has in mind when he speaks of tongues of angels but rather the intent of the speech when he writes, "And though I have the gift of prophecy, and understand all mysteries and all knowledge, and though I have all faith so that I could remove mountains but have not love, I am nothing." What Paul appears to be saying in these first two verses of 1 Corinthians 13 is not that there is a special class of angelic speech but that even if one is to speak with all the eloquence and wisdom available to man and even to the highest extent of the holy angels themselves who stand in the presence of God and behold all the glory and mysteries of heaven itself, but does not have love, then it amounts to nothing.

Some writers state that the tongue prayer language is not the language of angels at all but is speech prompted by the Holy Spirit uniquely created in each individual believer that is received from God at the time of salvation, the Spirit bringing the believer's own unique prayer language with His indwelling presence. This supernatural language is each believer's own special prayer venue, unlike anyone else's, and with this prayer language, the Spirit gets involved one-on-one with each believer in a unique and individual way, unfolding God's purpose and plan in the heart of the believer in a way they would not know otherwise. According to this view, the Holy Spirit knows God's plan for you and communicates this plan to you, which flows through you in the supernatural gift of tongues. This teaching is not found anywhere in the scriptures.

The Bible teaches that the intercessory ministry of the Holy Spirit is not a prayer language at all. It is the Holy Spirit communicating our hearts' desire to God as we pray, not as He prays through us. Nowhere in the Bible does it say the Holy Spirit prays for believers. The tongues-prayers might point to 1 Corinthians 14:14–15 for proof that the Holy Spirit prays for us, where Paul writes: "If I pray in a tongue, my spirit prays." In 1 Corinthians 14:15, he says the believer sings in the spirit, and in verse 16, the believer blesses in the spirit. They would argue that these verses confirm the practice of praying, singing, and blessing in a Holy Spirit–prompted language. However, the spirit Paul is referencing in these verses is not the Holy Spirit at all but the individual's human spirit.

The translators of the Bible made the correct interpretation by not capitalizing the word "spirit" to indicate this is not the Holy Spirit being referenced in these verses. The spirit (lower case) Paul is referring to is the inner desire, intentions, and emotions that make up our humanness. Other places in scripture, it is called the heart, as in Mark 12:30, "And you shall love the LORD your God with all your heart, with all your soul, with all your mind, and with all your strength. This is the first commandment." Jesus made mention of it when the disciples fell asleep in Gethsemane when He said, "the spirit is willing, but the flesh is weak." Paul states in 2 Corinthians 7:1, "Therefore, having these promises, beloved, let us cleanse ourselves from all filthiness of the flesh and spirit, perfecting holiness in the fear of God." This could not be speaking of the Holy Spirit since there is no filthiness in Him.

Paul further clarifies this distinction when he says in 1 Thessalonians 5:23, "Now may the God of peace Himself sanctify you completely; and may your whole spirit, soul, and body be preserved blameless at the coming of our Lord Jesus Christ." Paul concludes his argument in 1 Corinthians 14:15 by saying we are to sing, bless, and pray with both our inner desire and our minds, "What is the conclusion then? I will pray with the spirit, and I will also pray with the understanding. I will sing with the spirit, and I will also sing with the understanding." What Paul is saying is that we are to pray and sing with all our human capacities. A purely emotional experience is of little value without the mind understanding what is being said. The ministry of the Holy Spirit is always directed to the mind as well as to the spirit of the believer (2 Timothy 1:7).

Romans 8:26 states, "Likewise the Spirit also helps in our weaknesses. For we do not know what we should pray for as we ought, but the Spirit Himself makes intercession for us with groanings which cannot be uttered." This verse clearly states that the Spirit intercedes for us as we pray with nonverbal groanings, not some supernatural prayer language uttered by the Spirit so that God can communicate to the believer. In contrast, Dave Robertson, in his book on praying in tongues, states that "You can go into your room and pray…and God the Holy Spirit will create every single word that comes out of your mouth." This is not a teaching found in the Bible.

If, in fact, the tongues of angels refer to some angelic language prompted by the Spirit in believers or a Spirit language completely unique to every believer, then an interesting and somewhat defeating reality emerges when these utterances are analyzed across different cultures and language groups. Linguists have made exhaustive studies of various tongues spoken by Pentecostal groups from around the globe and discovered that the speaker would only make sounds consistent with their native language. D. A. Carson, in his exposition on 1 Corinthians, states, "When studies have been made of tongues made in different cultures, several startling conclusions have presented themselves. The tongues phenomena have been related to the speaker's natural language (e.g., a German or French tongues-speaker will not use one of the English "th" sounds, and English tongues-speakers will never use the "u" sound of French "cru")...very few tongues-speakers use two or more discreet patterns."

It would stand to reason that if tongues were indeed an angelic language prompted by the Spirit, then we would expect similar patterns of speech would occur across cultures reflecting the angelic pattern inherent in the heavenly language. Or if the language is unique to each individual believer, we would expect no discernable similarities at all. Studies have shown that the tongues patterns of individuals within a group are similar to one another, demonstrating a lack of individual uniqueness as would be expected if each Spirit language was unique to each believer as Robertson states.

In addition, each group varies from other groups with no discernable linguistic unity between groups. There would be an expectation of similarity between groups if the prayer languages were an angelic tongue. In other words, it appears that the sounds made by each group are consistent with learned sounds of the native languages of the group, not unlearned and prompted from a heavenly source.[19] These tongue sounds bear none of the elements of any true language but appear to be random sounds uttered in a random and repetitive fashion consistent within each group.

Another early study by W. A. Wolfram in 1966 observed that glossolalia, as practiced by various groups, lacks the basic elements of human language as a system of coherent communication. In a study comparing tongues speech and gibberish, that is, comparing the people purposefully making unintelligible sounds and people from different congregations speaking in supposed Spirit-induced tongues, it was discovered that the gibberish being spoken was consistently more diverse and complex than the tongues being spoken. It is the opposite one would expect if tongues were a heavenly-produced phenomenon, but it is consistent with a learned process that conforms to a particular group's expectations.[20]

Tongues proponents would argue that since tongues are God's language, normal human linguistics such as syntax, breath, phrasing, pause, context, structure, and other normal linguistic principles would not apply to speaking in tongues since God knows what God the Spirit through us is saying even if we don't. But if tongues are God's supernatural language to communicate His purpose and plan for each individual believer's life, as Robertson asserts, then how could it possibly benefit the believer if only God knows what is being said? Even after hours of tongues praying, the believer would have no greater understanding of God's purposes than at the beginning. Robertson would say the believer just knows in some mystical, mysterious transfer of knowledge which he fails to explain.

Some would argue that tongues are not a language at all but a supernatural tool of God for the purpose of communicating to the believer and, likewise, the believer to God in mystic communion. However, Paul clearly equates tongues with language in 1 Corinthians 14:9–10, where he states, "So likewise you, unless you utter by the tongue words easy to understand, how will it be known what is spoken? For you will be speaking into the air. There are, it may be, so many kinds of languages in the world, and none of them is without significance." Here, Paul makes clear that speaking in tongues is speaking in a known language of significance, which may require interpretation to edify the church. The word itself used for the tongue is "glossa" which means language. In the end, the Pentecostal attempt to establish a diversity of tongues on anything other than the understanding that tongues are known human languages causes the entire exegesis of the passages to break down into a labyrinth of Pentecostal confusion.

Another discrediting fact is that when separate individuals who self-proclaim the gift of interpretation of tongues are given an identical utterance to interpret, they give conflicting interpretations of the same utterance. The justification given for this is that God gives different interpretations to different individuals. This would imply that there is no cognitive unity in the utterance, but it is a purely subjective exercise with no linguistic cohesion. To the skeptic, both the utterance and the interpretation would appear to be a fabrication.

On one occasion, a professor interested in testing the validity of a tongues gathering, spoke a verse from the gospel of John in the original language of Greek, which he was confident the hearers would not know. The interpretation that came back had nothing in common with the actual translation of the verse. This by itself would not prove the false nature of the modern tongues phenomena, but it does, with the other evidence, show a pattern of inconsistency that should not be ignored. God is not the author of confusion (1 Corinthians 14:33).

Pentecostals assert that 1 Corinthians 12:10 validates the teaching that there are multiple gifts of tongues and multiple ways the gift of tongues is administered by the Holy Spirit. They assert that there is a public use of tongues and then a private use of tongues, a corporate use and a closet use, a prophetic use and a prayer use indicated by the phrase "to another different kind of tongues," the different kinds being indicative of the public and private manifestation of this gift. They might even concur that the restrictions and prohibitions placed on the exercise of this gift in Paul's instructions in 1 Corinthians 12:14 are indeed valid, but only for the public or corporate exercise of the gift, not for the private or prayer use of the gift.

For example, they say that the declaration not everyone speaks in tongues, as in 1 Corinthians 12:30, would indeed apply to the corporate gift of tongues, but they would also assert that the private use of a prayer language is available to all as it is a different kind of tongue. This would apply to the other limitations placed on this gift as well, such as women are not to speak in tongues in the church (1 Corinthians 14:34) or that there must be an interpreter (1 Corinthians 14:24) or no more than two or three are to speak in tongues and never at the same time (1 Corinthians 14:27), or that tongues should be used for the building up of the entire church and not just for personal edification (1 Corinthians 14:5). They would argue that the private or prayer use of tongues would not come under the same restrictions as the public use. And even though some Pentecostal groups might concur with these limitations in a public setting, very few

Pentecostal groups practice any of them. Instead, they allow the free public expression of tongues in the church without restriction. It is not at all unusual to see large numbers of people in Pentecostal congregations, both men and women, speaking and praying in tongues during a service or gathering without any interpretation in direct violation of scripture.

Chapter 4

Of Angels and Men

Regarding the "tongues of men and of angels" referenced in 1 Corinthians 13:1, we know that tongues of men refer to known human languages (1 Corinthians 14:9–10), which were created by God to set the boundaries of man's habitation (Acts 17:26–27) and to separate them because of corruption (Genesis 10:5; 11:1–7, Deuteronomy 32:8, Psalm 55:9). But nowhere in the Scripture does it refer to a unique angelic language or that there are multiple languages in heaven spoken by angels as the phrase "tongues of angels" (plural) would imply if the Pentecostal view were adopted. There certainly is no corruption in heaven to require holy angels to be separated by language. There is no scriptural evidence to suggest that holy angels speak a different language than fallen angels, as some Pentecostal literature states. Paul can't be saying that the "tongues of angels" are the multiplicity of languages in heaven, for there is no such reality taught in scripture as Psalm 103:20 states, "Bless the LORD, you His angels, who excel in strength, who do His word, Heeding the voice *(not voices)* of His word."

Tongues of angels can't be referring to an unknown tongues-prayer language because nowhere in scripture do angels speak without being fully understood by the hearer.

Angels are ministering spirits sent to minister to us (Hebrew 1:14) and, as such, speak so that we can understand their message. There is no direct statement or inference in scripture indicating that there is a special unknown angelic language of heaven.

Pentecostals would say that the heavenly language of 1 Corinthians 13:1 is the groanings of Romans 8:26 and that these groanings are the Spirit speaking this heavenly language to God through us. However, groaning is not a language and Romans 8:26 clearly states the Spirit's groanings are nonverbal sighs on our behalf. As such, the groanings can't scripturally be applied to the so-called prayer language of tongues or the heavenly language of angels. The word used for unutterable as applied to groaning in Romans 8:26 is the very simple Greek word *alaletos*; the "a" is the negative "not," and "laetos" to speak. It simply means not spoken or nonverbal. Whatever the Spirit's groanings are on our behalf, they are nonverbal and unuttered.

Regarding angels' language, Psalm 19:1–4 states that one of the purposes of the host of heaven is to declare the glory of God, and this would include the angelic host of heaven as well. Nehemiah 9:6 declares, "You alone are the Lord; You have made heaven, the heaven of heavens, with all their host, the earth and everything on it, the seas and all that is in them, and You preserve them all. The host of heaven worships You." The purpose of the heavenly host, including angels, is to declare God's glory in such a way so that we can understand, not in some obscure secret tongue but in a glorious, understandable declaration of worship.

Some argue that this supposed angel language is the pure language of Zephaniah 3:9, which God will one day restore upon His return. When one speaks in an unknown tongue, they argue, it is the language of heaven brought to earth, "For then I will restore to the peoples a pure language, that they all may call on the name of the LORD, to serve Him with one accord." But Zephaniah makes clear that what is being referenced is not a special angelic heaven language currently available to us in prayer, but a language of purity and holiness to be restored at His coming, not the corrupt speech of sin, as Isaiah says in 59:4. "No one calls for justice, nor does any plead for truth. They trust in empty words and speak lies; they conceive evil and bring forth iniquity."

In contrast, Zephaniah 3:13 says, "The remnant of Israel shall not do iniquity, nor speak lies; neither shall a deceitful tongue be found in their mouth: for they shall feed and lie down, and none shall make *them* afraid." The pure language of Zephaniah 3:9 is the language of righteousness, the pure language of a purified heart, cleansed and restored by the new covenant of Jeremiah 31:31–33: "Behold, the days are coming, says the LORD when I will make a new covenant with the house of Israel and with the house of Judah, not according to the covenant that I made with their fathers in the day *that* I took them by the hand to lead them out of the land of Egypt, My covenant which they broke, though I was a husband to them, says the LORD. But this is the covenant that I will make with the house of Israel after those days, says the LORD: I will put My law in their minds, and write it on their hearts, and I will be their God, and they shall be My people."

The final two verses, which are used by Pentecostal writers to prove the existence of distinct categories of tongues, are found in 1 Corinthians 12:10, "To another the working of miracles; to another prophecy; to another discerning of spirits; to another *divers* kind of tongues; to another the interpretation of tongues," and 1 Corinthians 12:28; "And God hath set some in the church, first apostles, secondarily prophets, thirdly teachers, after that miracles, then gifts of healings, helps, governments, diversities of tongues." In both verses, Paul references a diversity of tongues, which Pentecostal writers attribute to the supposed different categories of tongues, one restricted by the limitations of 1 Corinthians 14 and the other not restricted and available as a prayer language to all.

However, in verses 7–11 and 29–30 of chapter 12 and verse 34 of chapter 14, Paul makes clear that whatever diversities of tongues do exist, they are not available to all and are distributed by the sovereign act of the Holy Spirit only upon some believers as He wills. This directly contradicts the Pentecostal teaching that the prayer language aspect of tongues is available to all.

Another way Pentecostal writers attempt to circumvent the restrictions given in 1 Corinthians 14 is to artificially divide the gift of tongues by labeling them "known" tongues and "unknown" tongues. According to this division, known tongues would be known human language, and unknown tongues would be the heavenly angelic language or another kind of Spirit-induced prayer language. This is an artificial construct based on an unfortunate translation in the King James Bible. In various verses where tongues are discussed, the translators inserted the word "unknown," which is shown in italics in most Bibles before the word "tongue." The italics indicate that the word unknown does not appear in the original language. This has not stopped the Pentecostal writers from building an entirely false interpretation of this doctrine on this mistranslation. There is no scriptural basis for teaching the existence of an unknown tongue, only the existence of various kinds of known languages, as Paul confirms in 1 Corinthians 14:6–10: "But now, brethren, if I come to you speaking with tongues, what shall I profit you unless I speak to you either by revelation, by knowledge, by prophesying, or by teaching? There are, it may be, so many kinds of languages in the world, and none of them is without significance."

In an interesting footnote regarding the insertion of the word "unknown" before the singular "tongue" and the exclusion of "unknown" before the plural use "tongues," it is believed by scholars that this was done to draw a distinction between the legitimate gift of "tongues" which is defined in scripture as known languages, and the perverted use of an "unknown tongue" in the form of ecstatic gibberish being promoted by the Corinthians as a legitimate spiritual gift.

Chapter 5

The Spiritual Booster Shot

The most common proof text for the teaching of tongues as a Holy Spirit prayer language is found in Romans 8:26–27: "Likewise the Spirit also helps in our weaknesses. For we do not know what we should pray for as we ought, but the Spirit Himself makes intercession for us with groanings which cannot be uttered. Now He who searches the hearts knows what the mind of the Spirit is because He makes intercession for the saints according to the will of God." It is important to examine this passage carefully because it is the seminal text to validate the teaching of the tongues movement regarding praying in tongues. This is the key verse used to justify a Holy Spirit tongues-prayer language, so a proper understanding of what this verse teaches must be of primary importance to an understanding of the truthfulness of this core Pentecostal belief.

- "Likewise the Spirit." This would be a reference to the Holy Spirit.
- "Helps in our weaknesses. For we do not know what we should pray for as we ought." The weaknesses spoken of here are our inability to pray according to the will of God due to the corruption

in our flesh from sin. Paul says in 1 Corinthians 13:12 that we see through a glass darkly. 1 John 5:14 tells us that if we pray according to the will of God, He hears us. But because of the limitations of sin, we fall short of this reality in prayer, not always knowing what God's will is.

- "But the Spirit Himself makes intercession for us." Nowhere in this verse or anywhere else does the Bible teach that the Holy Spirit prays for believers or through believers. It is the Spirit Himself that ministers through His intercessory work. The pronoun "Himself" adds emphasis to the fact it is the Spirit alone that does this intercession. The word intercession is something done on our behalf, and it is something done for us. The word "for" is the Greek word ὑπέρ, which means on our behalf, not the word "dia," which means through us. Intercession is the unique work of God on our behalf, doing for us what we can't do for ourselves. Just as Christ intercedes for us as our High Priest advocating for us at God's right hand, so the Holy Spirit aids in Christ's High Priestly duties by interceding for us as we pray. This is not done through us but for us, on our behalf, "Therefore, He (Christ) is also able to save to the uttermost those who come to God through Him, since He always lives to make intercession for them" (Hebrew 7:25).

- "With groanings which cannot be uttered." The Spirit intercedes with groanings, not words or prayers, not languages known or unknown. Groanings means unverbalized sighs of emotion and petition from the Spirit to our high priest on our behalf. The word used regarding the Spirit's groanings is the simple Greek word *ἀλάλητος*, which is the combination of "a" or not, and "laleō" meaning to speak or emit a sound. The groanings of the Spirit are not verbalized. They can't be an angelic spirit language as claimed by the tongues crowd, as the scripture clearly states the groanings of the Spirit can't be verbalized,

- "Now He who searches the hearts." The one who searches the hearts is our high priest, the Lord Jesus Christ, who sits at God's right hand where His intercession on our behalf is performed. "and all the churches shall know that I am he which searcheth the reins and hearts" (Rev 2:23).
- "Knows what the mind of the Spirit is." The groanings on our behalf to our great high priest occur between the mind of the Spirit and the one who searches the heart. This is done for us, not through us, in some Spirit-inspired prayer language. There is no contribution on our part in view in this verse.
- "Because He makes intercession for the saints according to the will of God." Christ searches the heart, and the mind of the Holy Spirit communicates our heart's desire to do the will of God when we don't know what that will is because of the corruption of sin, not through our vocal cords but through the communion of the Spirit and Christ on our behalf

This verse teaches the opposite of what tongues advocates base their teaching on concerning a prayer tongues language. It is the opposite of what occurred on the day of Pentecost where the Spirit gave utterance to proclaim the gospel. In Romans 8:26, the Spirit's groanings are not utterable, not spoken, not verbalized, not prayers.

One variant of the interpretation that Romans 8:26 describes the prayer language view of tongues is the use of the phrase "praying in the Spirit" found in 1 Corinthians 14:2, Ephesians 6:18, and Jude 20. Some proponents of the prayer language interpretation of tongues assert that the phrase praying "in the spirit" is synonymous with praying in tongues   The webpage PentecostolTheology.com confirms this teaching by stating the following in their article, "Ten Reasons Why Speak in Tongues:" "Praying in tongues stimulates faith. 'But ye, beloved, building up yourselves on your most holy faith, praying in the Holy Ghost' (Jude 1:20 (KJV)." The widespread view among Pentecostals is that praying in the Spirit is synonymous with praying in tongues and teaching, which needs to be examined more closely.

According to tongues adherents, the phrase "praying in the Spirit" describes the Spirit praying through us in groanings, i.e., tongues as supposedly described in Romans 8:26, a teaching that we have already demonstrated has no scriptural basis. Additionally, examining the premise that praying in the Spirit is the same as praying in tongues and taking it to its logical conclusion becomes a preposterous and erroneous position and scripturally untenable. Ephesians 6:18 commands us as part of the armor of God that we pray always in the Spirit, the word "always" excluding any other way of praying. Those who assert that praying in the Spirit is synonymous with praying in a tongue prayer language must conclude then that we are commanded to always pray in tongues to fulfill the command of God given in the imperative to put on the whole armor of God, always praying in the Spirit. This, of course, is a ridiculous assertion and one that can't be justified biblically.

When faced with such a glaring theological inconsistency, Pentecostal teaching pivots to say that we indeed are to pray in the Spirit as Ephesians 6:18 instructs, but that can include praying in tongues but doesn't necessarily mean that we must pray in tongues. They seek to theologically have it both ways, and their literature promotes both contradictory views, one being that praying in the Spirit means praying in tongues and the other that praying in the Spirit can include praying in tongues. But neither view is scripturally sound since there is no basis in scripture to validate a private prayer language in tongues available to believers in the first place.

Praying in the Spirit simply means praying in the power of the Holy Spirit to accomplish the will of God through our prayers as commanded by 1 John 5:14. When we don't know what to pray for to accomplish His will, the Spirit intercedes for us with nonverbal "groanings" (Roman 8:26). We are required to pray because of the limitations of our mortal bodies, we have this treasure in earthen vessels as Paul states in 2 Corinthians 4:7. Jesus prayed while on earth due to taking on the likeness of men but without sin. The Holy Spirit faces no such limitation requiring the need to pray since He is one with the Father and the Son, and the Son, now glorified and seated at the right hand of God, needs no longer to pray as He has conquered all earthly limitations by His resurrection from the dead.

Chapter 6

Draw Me Close Oh Tongue

What would be the purpose of a secret prayer language if the one praying does not know what is being said? What exhortation or confidence in communion with God would be achieved in such an exercise? Proponents would respond by asking what is the purpose of a sunset, or the majestic thunder of waves or the expanse of the heavens? Just as those bring us closer to God's power and majesty, so too the process of speaking in tongues itself brings joy, ecstatic communion with God knowing that He is at work in you, fulfillment and satisfaction knowing the Spirit is moving on our behalf, bringing our prayers to His throne in a special way.

We all would covet those types of experiences, and if speaking or praying in tongues produced those results, then it would be hard to argue otherwise. However, there are multitudes that have come out of the tongues movement and have expressed just the opposite effect in their lives. Disillusion, dissatisfaction, depression, spiritual conflict, pride, the need to seek greater spiritual experiences to achieve the same emotional results, feelings of betrayal, spiritual shipwreck, demonic oppression, and abandonment of the faith are the telling results in many testimonies.[22]

George Gardiner, a pastor and former Pentecostal tongues speaker, writes this in his excellent book on the subject, "Sometimes the bizarre is introduced. I've seen people run around a room until they were exhausted. I've seen people climb tent poles, laugh hysterically, go into trances for days, and do other weird things as the high sought becomes more elusive. Eventually, there is a crisis, and a decision is made. He will sit in the back seats and be a spectator, fake it, or go on in the hope that everything will eventually be as it was. The most tragic decision is to quit and, in quitting, abandon all things spiritual as fraudulent. The spectators are frustrated, the fakers suffer guilt, the hoping are pitiable, and the quitters are a tragedy. No, such movements are not harmless."

Along with speaking in tongues, other supposed manifestations among Pentecostal groups attributed to the Holy Spirit include barking, screeching, and howling like animals, violent shaking of the head and body, acting as if drunk, i.e., drunk in the spirit, uncontrolled laughter, transportation to heaven to speak with Jesus, visitations from angels, uncontrollable burning as if by fire, and a host of other bizarre and often physically and emotionally harmful activities. These manifestations are not at all isolated events but are regular and celebrated experiences of the Pentecostal movement and its leaders.

The most satanic element of the tongues movement is the subordination of Scripture to the supposed revelations and prophetic utterances of the Spirit. This is not a peripheral issue but is a prominent characteristic of the Pentecostal movement. Many within the movement claim to receive direct inspiration and illumination under the guidance of the Holy Spirit which is why there is such a plethora of error within the movement when it comes to sound doctrine.

Many value their supposed revelations above the written Word of God. This also appears to have been occurring in Corinthians, where people supposedly under the direction of the Holy Spirit were calling Jesus accursed and not being rebuked for doing so (1 Corinthians 12:3). Apparently, the revelatory gifts were held in such high esteem that even when speaking blasphemies, they went unopposed, much like what occurs in Pentecostal groups of today.

Responding to criticism of the outlandish antics at Pentecostal gatherings, such as acting as if drunk, barking and howling like animals, leaders choking and slapping people in order to heal, pushing people over, standing on individuals, violently harmful shaking of the head and body, declaring visitations from angels in their presence, visions of Jesus appearing on stage, ignoring biblical mandates regarding the use of tongues, and other such activities, Michael Brown says in his book, *Authentic Fire: A Response to John MacArthur's Strange Fire*, "Yet when the real thing arrived—something I had prayed for and fasted for and longed for years—I embraced it with tears of joy while others mocked it." To be fair, Brown does criticize some of the excesses of the movement, but in a curious contradiction, he embraces the personalities and events where these excesses occur. Embracing events where clearly unbiblical practices and even demonic activity occur is often encouraged for the sake of unity.[23]

Those within the movement readily supplant sound Biblical teaching with Spirit-led utterances even when those utterances directly contradict scripture. The Bible warns believers to be on guard against seducing spirits that deceive with signs and wonders. It seems that the more sensational and outlandish the manifestation, the more readily it is received by tongues-speakers. In a recent example, the wife of self-proclaimed prophet Todd Bentley of GodTV fame from his extra-marital affair proclaimed the reception of a revelation from God in the form of a wild, radical, running, dancing elephant.[24] As she revealed the revelation of the elephant, she shook her head back and forth so violently it was difficult for her to speak. The whole event was received with applause and affirmation as a true revelation from God, even with the obvious lack of scriptural integrity. Such supplanting of biblical truth is common among Pentecostals, and it seems the more sensational the revelation, the more acceptance it receives.[25] Ultimately, the mistake of using emotional experience, good or bad, as a valid barometer of the truth is never a good practice. Jeremiah reminds us that the heart is desperately wicked and leads us astray (Jeremiah 17:9).

The tongues phenomenon and its excesses are certainly not unique to the Christian community. The same ecstatic Pentecostal experiences have been documented in the Hindu, Muslim, and many other modern-day religions. Felicitas D. Goodman, a psychological anthropologist and linguist, engaged in a study of various English-, Spanish-, and Mayan-speaking Pentecostal communities in the United States and Mexico. She compared tape recordings of non-Christian rituals from Africa, Borneo, Indonesia, and Japan as well, publishing her results in 1972 (*Speaking in Tongues: A Cross-Cultural Study in Glossolalia* by Felicitas D. Goodman, University of Chicago Press, 1972). Goodman concludes that "When all features of glossolalia were taken into consideration—that is, the segmental structure (such as sounds, syllables, phrases) and its suprasegmental elements (namely, rhythm, accent, and especially overall intonation—there is no distinction in glossolalia between Christians and the followers of non-Christian (pagan) religions."

Speaking in tongues was also a very common practice of the ancient pagan occult religions with similar frequency, intensity, and supposed euphoric effects as those in the tongues movement of today.[26] Satan is a master counterfeiter and deceiver, which is why we are commanded to study the word to show ourselves approved. We are to walk by the light and anchor of the word of God and not by any emotional, subjective experience. We are to walk by faith and not by sight.

Chapter 7

The Mystery of It All

The mystery religions of the ancient Greek and Roman world grew out of the need for the pagan populace to unite with their deities in a more real and experiential fashion. The ancient Greek religions and philosophies championed by Plato, Socrates, and Aristotle were a cerebral approach to an understanding of the gods of Mount Olympus. The gods were viewed as aloof and unattached to the mortal affairs of the world and were celebrated in an emotionally sterile form of worship. Rarely were the gods seen as approachable, and the populace hungered for personal worship and communion with their deities, one that was emotionally satisfying. Outside influences of worship from other cultures began to trickle into the Greek population and mindset. Persian, Phoenician, Syrian, Assyrian, Egyptian, and even mystic Jewish rituals gained significant followings among the Greeks, transforming their sterile worship into a vibrant interactive celebration where union with the gods could be achieved.

Local or national gods were seen as inadequate to meet the needs of a growing and diverse worldview. As one kingdom fell and was assimilated into a new one, the gods of the fallen were seen as impotent in defeat to the gods of the victor. Gods who were once worshipped were suddenly considered weak and possibly dead. This vacuum created a need to seek out new gods and new forms of worship that could fill the void. The old stale forms of worship were supplanted, and new and energizing deities and worship were embraced. As the populace embraced new gods and new ideas, the need for salvation, not in the Christian sense, but the personal release from their earthly condition, caused the mystery religions to proliferate.[27]

Through the mystery religions, the gods were no longer seen as distant inhabitants of some cosmic location, but worshipers could experience their presence by communion with the divine. These cults were not mysteries in the sense that they sought to uncover hidden divine truth available through research and common knowledge but were called mystery religions because the rites and rituals could only be discovered by being passed along from previous participants and were not to be revealed to anyone other than the devotees. Many ceremonies of the mystery religions were conducted at night, away from public view, in grottos, groves, and temples, and were closely guarded by armed sentinels. These secret rites or mysteries were so well guarded that very little of their actual activities had been recorded. Anyone found guilty of revealing the mysteries was punished with severe physical penalties, including death.

Mystery religions proliferated throughout the Greek and Roman world to such a degree that in every major town, day's long festivals and celebrations were held, initiating multitudes into various cults. It was not unusual for celebrations to occur one right after the other and often at the same time in the spring, causing conflict as the groups jostled for space and attention. Each mystery religion was dedicated to a particular god to be venerated. The best-known deities of these cults were Demeter, Dionysus (or Bacchus), and Apollo in Greece; Cybele and Attis in Phrygia; Mithra in Persia; Ishtar and Tammuz in Babylonia; Atargatis and Hadad in Cilicia; Ashtart and Eshmun [or Adon], the Aphrodite and Adonis of the Greeks; and Isis, Osiris, and Serapis in Egypt.[28] The military conquests of Alexander the Great and the Roman legions that came after gave rise to the dissemination of various cultic beliefs throughout the Greco-Roman world as people and ideas traversed the empires.

The rites of the mystery religions were organized and staged by clubs where people from all religious backgrounds and cultures were accepted. The rites and rituals were mostly symbolic and allegorical representations of the renewal of seasonal vegetative life and fertility as represented in the story of the gods. They reimagined the story of life, which made their appeal broad and diverse. The god of vegetation would die and experience rebirth, the god of fertility would mate with a partner and be played out by the priest and priestess, the god of the sun would rise from the netherworld and his trek retold as he makes his way across the heavenly obstacles bringing new life to the earth, a celestial champion would vanquish a bull and revive men by having them bath in its blood.[29] As Angus states in his book, *The Mystery-Religions and Christianity*, "All of this was transmuted to serve as a paradigm of man's situation, of his own death and revival, his own illumination, and the infusion into him of new blood." Allegiance to local or state gods was replaced by a personal form of worship to gods and ideas that were universal.[30]

The appeal of the mysteries was not wholly religious. There were different levels of investment among the participants, as there are in many modern religions. Some of the inductees drank deeply from the mystery well, being fully immersed in communion with the gods and the euphoria that it produced. Others were drawn by the spectacle of the festivities and music, the carnival atmosphere, and the colorful crowds, while still others were drawn to the feasts, the drinking, and the orgies. It could be said that there was something for everyone in the mystery religions, which gave them broad appeal.

Most of the mystery religions followed a similar pattern in their public and private worship activities. The first day of what usually was a three-day celebration would be a time of dedication for those to be inducted into the cult. There would be the inductee's time of prayer and fasting followed by a procession to the ocean or holy fountain for ceremonial cleansing and more prayer. Vows would be spoken, magical incantations, and speeches made by the priests and dignitaries, followed by a solemn night of meditation.

The second day would be the official procession through the streets of the city to the temple, where the rituals would be performed. In the procession would be the priests, the previously inducted devotees, and official stewards chosen to carry the physical artifacts to be used in the secret ceremony. These artifacts consisted of items that were used in proclaiming the mysteries and the retelling of the god's significance to the worshipper. Each god had a story associated with their life, their interaction with other gods, and with mortals. These artifacts were used to retell their story and appease the gods to entice their presence and to coax them into interaction with the ceremonies.

The procession would include loud music, clanging cymbals, chanting, beating of drums, dancing semi-nude priestesses, carrying of burning torches, incense, colorful attire, banners, sacrificial animals, and other items, which produced a carnival-like atmosphere. Once at the temple or place of worship, more ceremonial cleansing, long petitions, prayers, and magic incantations would be offered, inviting the presence of the gods. The sacrifice of bulls and other animals would be made and would later be used in the love feast that would follow. In the evening, a lavish feast of sacrificed animals along with intoxicating drinks would be served. The night's festivities would often conclude with an orgy of various sorts of immorality and debauchery to attract the attention of the gods and entertain the participants. The gods themselves were seen as lustful and immoral, and the orgies served as a means of uniting with the divine.

On the third day, the inductees would be led to a secret location where the mysteries were revealed to the participants, and induction into the cult would be finalized. These rituals, for the most part, are still unknown as the participants were very diligent not to reveal their secrets. These rituals had a profound effect on the participants as it was common for demonic supernatural activity to be manifested at these inductions. Physical manifestations supposedly attributed to the presence of the gods included speaking in tongues, trancelike states of ecstasy, levitation, healings, violent shakings, prophetic utterances, supernatural apparitions, bright flashing lights, and loud voices, which produced terror and wonder among the inductees. So profound were these ceremonies on the participants that in one instance, an inductee was so overcome that he self-castrated as a sign of devotion to the deity. This became a regular part of the worship of the deity Cybele, and many subsequent devotees called Gallus followed this example, devoting themselves exclusively to her service.[31] For the most part, the mystery cults were not formal methods of moral instruction but a loose brotherhood of like-minded followers whose interest was in the sensual and communal characteristics of the mysteries. The rites were designed to stimulate the imagination and to awaken a vivid sense of both the terrors and joys that lie beyond their earthly pilgrimage.[32]

One of the most egregious mysteries was the Dionysos cult. Dionysos, also known as Bacchus, was the god of wine and mirth, and the followers of Dionysos certainly lived up to the name. Their behavior was so reprobate that, according to Livy in his History of Rome,[33] they were expelled from Rome by the decree of the Roman senate. This cult featured female priestesses and devotees known as Bacchae, who participated half-naked in the public processions, gyrating sensually to chants and to the rhythm of the drums, flutes, and cymbals. They were known to tear apart live animals limb from limb and devour the raw meat as Dionysos was torn apart by the Titans.[34] Inebriated by wine and possibly demonic possession and under the hypnotic effects of the procession, the Bacchae would engage in speaking in tongues and would lead the orgies that followed the love feast into violent and brutal immorality visited upon men, women, and children of all ages. If anyone refused to be violated, they would be removed from the festivities and perhaps murdered. The Roman senate eventually banned participation in this cult, but the publicity and notoriety only caused a greater interest and increased its popularity.[35]

Into this world, the gospel of grace and the transforming power of Jesus Christ entered, bringing salvation and deliverance. But the transition was not without its difficulties as the converts brought with them some of the trappings of their previous pagan culture and religious practices as was the case in Corinth.

Chapter 8

Gotta Do It

In the article "The Sound of Speaking in Tongues (Everything You Need to Know)," author Jeran Ferguson makes this assertion regarding tongues, "So the fact that this language is a mystery that no one can understand proves that tongues is a language for you and God only. The Holy Spirit is inspiring your utterance uniquely so that you can communicate with God *in a way that others can't*" (emphasis added). What this author is saying is that only by speaking or praying in tongues can a Christian experience full access and complete communication with our Heavenly Father. Unless a person speaks in tongues, they have limited their access to God.

This teaching is at the core of the modern tongues movement, that to experience the fullness of God and to access the complete ministry of the Holy Spirit, one must speak in tongues or miss out on the full spiritual benefits that God has for the believer. This core viewpoint of the tongues movement is demonstrated in a tract written by a well-known Pentecostal minister, R. E. McAlister, and published by the Gospel Publishing House, Springfield, Missouri. In Evangel Tract No. 251, he writes, "It is admitted by Bible students the world over that speaking with tongues as the Spirit gives utterance is a sign. Suppose we ask the question, 'Of what is it a sign?' The answer is found in God's own Word, for we find the sign accompanied by the reception of the Holy Spirit when God standardized the New Testament Christian experience. It follows logically, then, that only those who have spoken in tongues can lay claim to a normal New Testament experience. All others, regardless of what they profess or claim, ARE BELOW PAR." Here, McAlister makes a confession few Pentecostals are willing to make that speaking in tongues was a sign. But he then ignores the clear declaration of Paul in 1 Corinthians 14 that tongues were a sign to unbelieving Jews and makes a completely unfounded conclusion that tongues were a sign of normal New Testament experience.

Pentecostal writer Dave Robertson, in his book on speaking in tongues, confirms this belief by stating, "Every one of us is supposed to receive this operation because if we ever are to come into the unity of the faith, we must learn how to release the power of the Holy Spirit, our teacher who dwells inside of us. He is more than willing to pray hour after hour in divine secrets and mysteries before the Father to help us prepare spiritually for the operation to which God separated us at our rebirth."[36] The obvious problem with this logic is that in only three instances in Acts is the Spirit associated with speaking in tongues. The first was on the day of Pentecost, the second was in Acts 10 with the conversion of Cornelius, and the third in Acts 19 with the conversion of the Ephesian disciples of John the Baptist. With every other conversion or filling of the Spirit mentioned in the book of Acts, there is no mention of tongues speaking (Act 2, Acts 3, Acts 4, Acts 8, Acts 9, Acts 13, Acts 16, Acts 17, Acts 18, and Acts 21). Why would only three instances of speaking in tongues "standardize Christian New Testament experience" to the exclusion of a far greater number of occurrences where tongues did not occur? If the number of occurrences sets the standard for Christian experience, it would stand to reason the real standard would be the majority of instances where tongues were not spoken. Tongues advocates would argue that just because tongues were not mentioned doesn't mean that they weren't present. Support for such a specious argument is both biblically unattainable and exegetically unsound.

To say, as some tongues-speakers do, that praying in tongues is not a spiritual requirement but only a divine benefit available to believers is to deny the teaching of Pentecostal literature. Many writers assert that praying in tongues is, in fact, a requirement to demonstrate the believer's baptism by the Holy Spirit and to access fully the divine benefits afforded the believer. The Word of God is clear that there are no below-par believers but that we all have received the full benefits of God's grace in salvation. Speaking or praying in tongues is not a requirement to realize this grace or to gain superior access to the Father. Unity is achieved as we grow in knowledge, not through some divine, mystical experience (Ephesians 4:13).

- *We have all received the baptism of the Holy Spirit at salvation.* "For by one Spirit are we all baptized into one body, whether we be Jews or Gentiles, whether we be bond or free; and have been all made to drink into one Spirit" (1 Corinthians 12:13).
- *We all have been given every spiritual blessing.* "Blessed be the God and Father of our Lord Jesus Christ, who has blessed us with every spiritual blessing in the heavenly places in Christ" (Ephesians 1:3).
- *We are complete in Christ.* "And you are complete in Him, who is the head of all principality and power" (Colossians 2:10).

- *We are lacking in nothing.* "But let patience have its perfect work, that you may be perfect and complete, lacking nothing."
- *We all have full access to the throne of God.* "Let us therefore come boldly to the throne of grace, that we may obtain mercy and find grace to help in time of need" (Hebrew 4:13).
- *We are made perfect in Christ.* "For by one offering He has perfected forever those who are being sanctified" (Hebrews 10:14).
- *We are made complete through the word of God, not through a mystic experience.* "All Scripture is given by inspiration of God, and is profitable for doctrine, for reproof, for correction, for instruction in righteousness, that the man of God may be complete, thoroughly equipped for every good work."
- *We have been given everything we need.* "As His divine power has given to us all things that pertain to life and godliness, through the knowledge of Him who called us by glory and virtue" (2 Peter 1:3).
- *Every believer has full access to God.* "For through Him we both have access by one Spirit to the Father" (Ephesians 2:18); "In whom we have boldness and access with confidence through faith in Him" (Ephesians 3:12).

There are no second-class citizens of heaven separated by speaking or not speaking in tongues. Nowhere in scripture does it teach that there is something we must do to receive more of what God has graciously provided every believer. This is truly a doctrine of demons, the equivalent of Satan's first lie in the Garden.

Chapter 9

Pray For Me, For Me

Another one of the core teachings of the tongues movement is that the gift of speaking or praying in an unknown tongue is appropriate and encouraged for the benefit of personal edification. In fact, self-edification is considered the chief benefit of speaking and praying in tongues. Speaking and praying in tongues, they say, benefits the believer in ways unavailable to those not speaking in tongues. The main verses used to bolster this teaching are found in 1 Corinthians 14:2, 4–5, and 14–15. From these verses the tongues apologists attempt to draw various principles that are benefits of speaking and praying in an unknown tongue. These principles include the use of tongues for spiritual growth and ecstasy, the use of tongues for speaking directly to God through a special venue, the use of tongues to enter spiritual mysteries not experienced apart from speaking in tongues, a deeper union with the Holy Spirit and our spirit, the ability to pray perfectly by being overtaken by the power the Holy Spirit because when you speak or pray in tongues, you are talking to God by divine, supernatural means, and the ability to know more perfectly God's plan and purpose for your life. They assert that praying or speaking with other tongues is praying or speaking as the Spirit gives utterance; therefore, it is Spirit-directed utterance. Although noble goals, the spiritual gift of glossa or languages was never intended to accomplish any of these benefits.

The reality was not that Paul was commending the Corinthian church on their pursuit of the benefits of self-edification through speaking in tongues but that he was attempting to move them away from the pagan ecstasies of the occult mystery religions that had permeated and perverted the legitimate practice of the true spiritual gift of glossa. As John MacArthur points out, "This was a very common thing in their culture. So the term used in Corinthians, *glōssais lalein*, to speak in tongues, was not invented by Bible writers but was a term used commonly in the Greco-Roman culture to speak of pagan ecstasy, and going out of the body, connecting with the deity, and in a mystical way beginning to speak the language of the gods, which came out as some kind of gobbledygook and gibberish."[37]

The Corinthian church had substituted the reemergence of pagan idol worship into their thinking and incorporated a semi-sanitized version of the cult practices around them, including baptizing people for the dead (1 Corinthians 15:29), which was a pagan practice that allowed relatives to affect the eternal condition of their departed ancestors. The belief that the living could benefit the dead is an idea that Plato comments on in his work "Republic, Book 2.6–7:" "And mendicant prophets go to rich men's doors and persuade them that they have a power committed to them by the gods of making an atonement for a man's own or his ancestor's sins by sacrifices or charms, with rejoicings and feasts; and they promise to harm an enemy, whether just or unjust, at a small cost; with magic arts and incantations binding heaven…according to which they perform their ritual…that expiations and atonements for sin may be made by sacrifices and amusements…and are equally at the service of the living and the dead."

This belief that the living can affect the dead is still with us today in the Papal Church. Let me explain by personal illustration. When my father, who was a devout Catholic, died in a sudden accident, the church approached my mom with an offer to conduct a special mass for the purpose of reducing the time my father would have to spend in purgatory. For those unfamiliar with this teaching of the Catholic church, let me explain. According to Catholic doctrine, when a person dies, they must spend time in purgatory to pay the penalty for and purge the residual sin that Christ's death did not satisfy. Purgatory is much like the suffering of hell but without being eternal. Once the individuals' residual sins are purged, the suffering believer can enter eternal bliss. According to the church, this special mass would help reduce the suffering and time my father would have had to spend in purgatory. Of course, this came with a steep price, which my mom was unable to pay, and therefore, the mass was not held. What a cruel hoax to perpetrate upon a grieving spouse for the sake of greed.

These and other pagan practices had inculcated the church in Corinth and were gross errors. There is little doubt that the Gentile converts of Corinth would have been very familiar with these pagan practices, such as baptizing for the dead and speaking in tongues, since many pagan festivals were conducted in Corinth[38] and one of the most import-ant pagan temples of Greece, the Temple of Apollo and the Oracle of Delphi, was located just across the gulf from Corinth. Almost every major polis in Greece had temples that celebrated festivals dedicated to the gods, and Paul was attempting to persuade the Corinthians away from the cult practices of the mystery religions of the day and into a better understanding.

Along with speaking in unknown tongues, other cult excesses included sexual immorality, uncontrollable ecstasy, dancing in a frenzy of excitement, crashing of loud cymbals, screeching flutes, intoxicating love feasts, tearing apart live animals and eating raw meat, being baptized in the blood of sacrificed bulls, and other chaotic and disorderly conduct for the purpose of gaining entrance into a special union with the gods. Some of these practices had undoubtedly infiltrated the church at Corinth along with the tongues error. The church had turned a legitimate spiritual gift into a cult-like practice designed to fulfill the selfish pursuit of a higher spiritual experience.

In no sense should the Corinthian Church be seen as a model of Christian experience and practice. Although outstanding in many ways, the church was an immature and carnal church that had allowed the cultural practices of their pagan surroundings and upbringings to continue influencing their behavior. They had allowed celebrity worship to enter, which Paul addressed in chapter one. They had left their reliance on the Holy Spirit, which Paul addressed in chapter two. In chapter three, Paul had to correct the divisions and envious squabbles that had developed in the church. Immorality had made its way into the church in chapter six. They were defrauding one another and suing each other in the pagan courts in chapter seven. They had tarnished the institution of marriage in chapter eight, and Paul had to battle their selfish indulgence in chapters eight and nine. In chapter ten, Paul had to address the idiolatry that was creeping back into the church, and in chapter eleven, Paul had to guide them in the proper way to function in the church. They had perverted the exercise of spiritual gifts and needed stern correction in chapters twelve to fourteen, and they were confused about the teachings concerning the resurrection. In every instance, the Corinthians were having problems that needed apostolic attention and correction. Their misunderstanding regarding the exercise of the gift of tongues was no exception.

It would be wrong to think that this vibrant urban church was without virtue. It should be remembered that the Apostle Paul also commended their numerous outstanding qualities, such as the following:

- They were true believers in Christ (1 Corinthians 1:2)
- They had all the spiritual gifts functioning in the body (1 Corinthians 1:7)
- They had a rich knowledge of the word (1 Corinthians 1:5)
- They were a faithful church, desiring to do what was right (1 Corinthians 7:1, 11:2)
- They were a repentant church (2 Corinthians 2:6–7, 7:9)
- They were a persevering church (2 Corinthians 1:7)
- They were a praying church (2 Corinthians 1:11)
- They were a forgiving church (2 Corinthians 2:10)
- They were a welcoming church (2 Corinthians 7:13)
- They were a generous church (2 Corinthians 9:1–2)
- They were a prosperous church (2 Corinthians 9:10–11)
- They were an affectionate church (2 Corinthians 13:12)

It would be equally wrong to label all Pentecostal believers as corrupt and without virtue. Just like the church in Corinth, there are many wonderful believers in such churches who have been led astray by false teaching into unprofitable practices. We should be praying for them as Paul did in Ephesians 1:18: "The eyes of your understanding being enlightened; that you may know what is the hope of His calling, what are the riches of the glory of His inheritance in the saints."

Chapter 10

The Jesus Prayer Method

In Matthew 6:7, Jesus condemned the pagan prayer practices of his day, "And when you pray, do not use vain repetitions as the heathen *do.* For they think that they will be heard for their many words." The word used to translate "vain repetitions" in the King James Bible (KJV) is translated more accurately as "don't babble on" in the New Living Translation, "do not keep on babbling" in the New International Version, and "empty phrases" in the English Standard Version. The pagan prayers often included the practice of speaking in tongues, as evidenced by the ancient *Mithras Liturgy*, a prayer guide for the pagan worship of Mythra, which included magical components, descriptions of breathing techniques, recipes, magical rites, amulets, and magical words of power (*voces magicae*), or *glossolalic* (speaking in tongues).

According to Vine's Expository Dictionary of New Testament Words, the Greek word *battalegeo*, which the KJV translates as "vain repetitions" in Matthew 6:7, "Is probably from an Aramaic phrase and onomatopoeic in character. The rendering of the Sinaitic Syriac is 'Do not be saying *battalatha*, idle things,' i.e., meaningless and mechanically repeated phrases, the reference being too pagan (not Jewish) modes of prayer." To describe a word as being onomatopoeic means that the word is descriptive of a sound, such as the word zip or fizz. What the Lord Jesus is saying is don't pray by repeating empty sounds like the pagans. The words in Matthew 6:7 most likely condemn the pagan mystery religions and their use of ecstatic gibberish and empty babbling in prayer communion with their deities. Instead, we are instructed by the Lord to use clear and meaningful language to communicate with our Heavenly Father, "Our Father in heaven, hallowed be your name." On the contrary, the prayers of the pagans to their gods were tedious, aggrandizing, and repetitive and sought to appeal to the vanity and ego of the deity to secure their blessing and favor. The prayers were replete with accolades of the god's greatness and power and were appeals for attention and favor by flattery and persuasion, and repetitive meaningless sounds.

Another aspect of pagan prayer that Jesus's admonition addressed was the contrast between the impersonal nature of the pagan deities and our heavenly Father. Unlike the believer's relationship with a loving and caring Father, the deities of the pagans were impersonal, self-centered, and ego-driven, with little interest in the affairs of mortals except to satisfy their own lust for power or personal pleasure. The prayers, rites, and convocations of the pagans were a means to coerce and cajole these self-centered deities to be mindful of the devotees and their requests. This pagan attempt to draw concern from the gods is clearly illustrated by Elijah's confrontation with the pagan prophets of Baal in 1 Kings 18:26–29 as they tried to attract the attention of their gods by loud petition and self-mutilation, two common cult practices. On the contrary, believers have no such requirement as our God knows what we need even before we ask and desires to give good things to His children as a loving and concerned Father.

A main element of pagan worship was festivals with large gatherings in which elaborate rituals and cacophonous noise and prayers were offered to summon the attention of the gods and to stir the people to heightened levels of excitement and abandon. The use of loud cymbals, drums, dancing, sexual immorality, sacrifices, and scripted prayers were necessary to force the attention of the gods. So vital were these activities to the process that if they were not done in the exact prescribed sequence, the priests would be required to begin the day long process over again from the start so as not to incur the wrath of the gods. Our Lord instructed His followers not to pray in this fashion but to pray in secret, and our Father in secret will reward us openly.

In like fashion, many Pentecostal writers encourage praying in tongues as a means of praying more effectively and to enter a more personal mode of communion with our heavenly Father. Since tongues supposedly are the Holy Spirit praying through us and for us, it garnishes greater attention and response from God than we would otherwise secure. No such teaching is found in Scripture but, in fact, was a common element of pagan prayer practices that the Lord Jesus warned against.

Chapter 11

Are We There Yet?

In many ways the church in Corinth was a church full of wonderful believers standing as a testimony for Christ in a godless city. But the church in Corinth still needed to receive instruction, and to be admonished to pursue sound doctrine and conduct. They weren't where they needed to be as far as sound understanding and practice were concerned. The church had grown rapidly and drew converts from a variety of backgrounds and past immoral practices (1 Corinthians 6:9–11). Some of these practices had resurfaced in their pursuit of spiritual gifts, and the apostle was attempting to gently move them away from these distorted practices.

> "I am writing this to you before I come, hoping that I won't need to deal severely with you when I do come. For I want to use the authority the Lord has given me to strengthen you, not to tear you down" (2 Corinthians 13: 10).

Like a concerned parent coaxing a wayward child to abandon unprofitable behavior, the Apostle exhorted the Corinthian church in the following passages. These passages have been used by Pentecostal writers to try and demonstrate Paul's acceptance of the Corinthians' use of tongues. However, it is more accurate to say that while acknowledging their error, he was providing alternative practices that would more perfectly edify the believers.

The legitimate gift of tongues was indeed operating in the church at Corinth. There were some who had the ability to speak in a human language, not their own, through the power of the Holy Spirit. There were also those who had the gift of interpretation of that language as well. The purpose of those gifts was to proclaim the message of God to the church for its edification and as a sign to unbelievers that the power of God was with His church. However, it is apparent from Paul's exhortations that those with this gift had begun to use it for selfish purposes. Speaking in tongues had become a sign of exalted spirituality, and others began to imitate this practice for self-promotion. Rather than try and determine the true exercise of the gift from the false that existed in the Church, Paul gave principles for all to follow in the exercise of the gift for the benefit of the entire body.

"For he who speaks in a tongue does not speak to men but to God, for no one understands him; however, in the spirit he speaks mysteries" (1 Corinthians 14:2). Without an interpretation, the language being spoken by the one with the true gift of tongues was not benefiting the church. They were exercising the gift in a way that only God could understand, for no one else would know what was being spoken. It would be a mystery to them. This practice became an unprofitable use of the gift for personal aggrandizement.

This was also a pagan practice of the cults in their quest for a higher union with the divine. The pagan practice of speaking in tongues was a sign that union with the gods had been achieved. This is not a commendation by Paul but is the premise of his correction that follows in verse 3; "But he that prophesieth speaketh unto men to edification, and exhortation, and comfort."

Four more times in chapter 14, in verses 4, 5, 12, and 26, Paul reminds the brethren that selfish pursuit and exhibition are not the goals of spiritual gifts. All spiritual gifts, including glossa, are given for the edification of others. Paul emphasizes this clearly in verses 4 and 5, where he writes,

> He who speaks in a tongue edifies himself, but he who prophesies edifies the church. I wish you all spoke with tongues, but even more that you prophesied; for he who prophesies is greater than he who speaks with tongues, unless indeed he interprets, that the church may receive edification.

Paul is clearly emphasizing the fact that prophecy is superior to the gift of tongues. Prophecy, as used here, is the preaching and teaching of God's word more than the predicting of future events. The emphasis on proclaiming God's truth should always be a priority over tongues, as Paul exhorted a young protégée, Timothy, "Preach the word! Be ready in season and out of season. Convince, rebuke, exhort, with all longsuffering and teaching" (2 Timothy 4:2). Paul makes this clear in 1 Corinthians 14: 13, "Yet in the church I would rather speak five words with my understanding, that I may teach others also, than ten thousand words in a tongue." This truth is often lost in our modern Pentecostal gatherings which place an exorbitant amount of emphasis on tongues and signs and wonders to the exclusion of just about everything else.

> For if I pray in a tongue, my spirit prays,
> but my understanding is unfruitful.
> What is the conclusion then? I will pray
> with the spirit, and I will also pray with
> the understanding. I will sing with the
> spirit, and I will also sing with the under-
> standing. (1 Cor 14:14–15)

When Paul says, "My spirit prays," in the verse above, he is not saying that the Holy Spirit is praying on our behalf but that our human spirit is praying without the benefit of our mind comprehending what is being spoken. This is not an encouragement to sing and pray in tongues for personal fulfillment but an admonishment to exercise the gift for the benefit of all. Without the mind understanding what is spoken, the gift had become unprofitable. This was also a cult practice, the act of uniting with the divine by voiding the mind of any conscience thought and allowing the presence of the gods to move the individual into an ecstatic state. This ecstatic state was accomplished by loud rhythmic music, the crashing of cymbals and beating of drums, darkness and flashing lights, and frenzied dancing. These had the effect of producing a semi-hypnotic state in the participants and would commonly be evidenced by speaking in the language of the gods. This was quite common among the Bacchae of the Dionysos mystery religion. The Bacchae were female devotees who would become frenzied and speak in unknown tongues, a practice Paul forbids the women in the Corinthian church to engage in (1 Corinthians 14:34).

The pagan practice of removing cognitive barriers, as would occur in an ecstatic state, is also a fundamental requirement of the tongues movement to allow your spirit and emotions to enter union with the Holy Spirit. Charles and Frances

Hunter, who traveled across the world in healing explosion meetings where as many as fifty thousand attended, said this as part of their curriculum teaching people how to speak in tongues, "The reason some of you don't speak fluently is that you try to think of the sounds. So when we pray this prayer, and you start speaking in your heavenly language, don't try to think…You don't even have to think in order to pray in the spirit." This is in direct opposition to the commands of scripture given in Paul's instruction and elsewhere. We are to worship God with all our heart, soul, mind, and strength.

It is important to remember that scripture instructs us that the exercise of any spiritual gift is not for the personal edification of the individual but for the building up of the body as a whole. Although a person may profit from the exercise of their gift, that is not the primary purpose of spiritual gifts. The exercise of spiritual gifts in the church is likened to the operation of the human body. Each member is given a spiritual capacity to function in the body, and each member of the body contributes to the body's health as a whole. The hand does not exist for the purpose of the hand, nor does the eye does operate for the purpose of the eye only, but contributes to the proper functioning of the body of which it is a part. But in its function as part of the body, it benefits as well from the health of the whole, as Paul states in Ephesians 4:16; "From whom the whole body, joined and knit together by what every joint supplies, according to the effective working by which every part does its share, causes growth of the body for the edifying of itself in love." "The eagerness of the Corinthians for showy spiritual manifestations constantly needed the sobering corrective of "the good of others" pressed upon them."[39]

Wrap It Up

One of the glaring problems in the church at Corinth was that the gift of tongues was being used in a selfish and divisive manner, being patterned after the mystery religions of their day. Paul was writing to correct that problem. They were carnal and immature in their understanding of spiritual gifts in general and were exercising what they believed was the gift of tongues in a way that was becoming detrimental to the edification of the church. Instead of building up the body, they were causing division and confusion, even becoming an obstacle to the furtherance of the gospel as Paul exhorts them in 1 Corinthians 14:23, "Therefore if the whole church comes together in one place, and all speak with tongues, and there come in those who are uninformed or unbelievers, will they not say that you are out of your mind?" Paul was not commending them for their use of tongues as a means of personal edification. He was correcting their misuse of this gift for selfish exhibition instead of its intended purpose, for the edification of the church which is the purpose of all spiritual gifts. No spiritual gift is given solely for personal edification. In the case of the Corinthian church, the exercise of the gift had become unprofitable. Their exercise of what they believed about the gift of tongues was becoming disruptive and divisive and needed correction.

Endnotes

1   Stolee, H. 1963. *Speaking in Tongues*, 1st ed., pp. vii-viii. Augsburg Publishing House.

2   MacArthur, John. "The Truth About Tongues Part 1 and 2." Sermon, Grace Community Church, June 9 and 16, 1977.

3   Horton, G. and Shimron, Y. 2017. "Southern Baptists Change Policy on Speaking in Tongues." April 30, 2024. http://www.hughesnews.com.

4   This occurred in the writers Sunday school class in a Southern Baptist Church in Alabama in 2024.

5   Stolee, H. 1963. *Speaking in Tongues*, 1st ed., pp. vii-viii. Augsburg Publishing House.

6   Blare, L. 2021. "Appalachian snake handlers put their faith in God—And increasingly, doctors." www.christianpost.com.

7   Shah, D. 2023. "What Is the Law of First Mention. NCESC. April 30, 2024. http://www.ncesc.com.

8   Joyner, R. n. d. The History and Future of the Present Revival, Part 1. Morning Star Ministries. April 30, 2024. http://www.morningstgarministries.org.

9   Ghringhetli, S. 2008. Bentley, GodTV Back on the Air in Lakeland, Florida. Charisma News. April 30, 2024. http://cn.mycharisma.com.

10   Apologetics Index. 2008. Todd Bentley: Exposed on ABC Nightline; Takes a Break. http://www.apoligeticsindex.org/699-todd-bentley-exposed-on-abc-nightline-takes-a-break.

11   *Christianity Today*. 2020. "Todd Bentley Investigation Finds "Steady Pattern" of Immoral Conduct." http://www.christianitytoday.com/news/2020/january/todd-bentley-charismatic-preacher-investigation-misconduct.html.

12   Got Questions Ministries. 2022. "What is the latter rain movement? Got Questions." April 30, 2024. http://www.gotquestions.org.

13 Stolee, H. 1963. *Speaking in Tongues*, 1st ed., pp. vii-viii. Augsburg Publishing House.

14 Jay, E. G. 1976. *The New Testament Greek: An Introductory Grammer* (4th ed., pp. 5–6). London: SPCK

15 MacArthur, J. (1992). *Charismatic Chaos* (1st ed.). Zondervan Publishing House.

16 Robertson, D. (1999). *The Walk of the Spirit, the Walk of Power: The Vital Role of Praying in Tongues*, 1st ed., p. 377. Dave Robertson Ministries.

17 Robertson, D. (1999). *The Walk of the Spirit, the Walk of Power: The Vital Role of Praying in Tongues*, 1st ed., p. 12. Dave Robertson Ministries.

18 Derby Media Group. 2004. "Speaking in Tongues." William Branham Historical Research. https://william-branham.org/site/research/topics/speaking_in_tongues.

19 Frank, A. A. (1998). "Tongue-Speech and Gibberish: An Exploration and Comparison" (Master's Thesis, Brynwamr). https://www.scholarship.tricolib.brynmawr.edu.

20 Ferguson, J. 2020. "Praying in the Spirit versus praying in tongues. What is the difference?" http://www.pursuingthetruth.org.

21 Stolee, H. 1963. *Speaking in Tongues*, 1st ed., pp. 62–69. Augsburg Publishing House.

22 Brown, M. (2015). *Authentic Fire: A Response to John Macarthur's Strange Fire*, 1st ed., pp. 245–246. Mary Lake Florida; Creation House.

23 "Todd Bently and Wife's Big Radical Elephant Prophecy." n.d. April 19, 2024. https://www.youtube.com/watch?v=fxokQizmGAE.

24 Reagan, D. D. n.d. "An Evaluation of the Florida Healing Ourtpouring. Lamb and Lion Mininstries." http://www.christianprophecy.org.

25 Stolee, H. 1963. *Speaking in Tongues*, 1st ed., pp. 18–19. Augsburg Publishing House.

26 Angus, S. (1966). *The Mystery Religions and Christianity*, 1st ed., pp. 12–13. University Books, New Hyde Park, New York.

27 Case, Shirley, (1914) *Christianity and the Mystery Religions*, 1st ed., p. 8. The Biblical World.

28 Case, Shirley, (1914) *Christianity and the Mystery Religions*, 1st ed., p. 8. The Biblical World.

29 Reitzenstein, Richard. 1978. *Hellenistic Mystery-Religions: Their Basic Ideas and Significance*, pp. 42–43. Pittsburgh: Pickwick Press.

30 Angus, S. (1966). *The Mystery Religions and Christianity*, 1st ed., pp. 196–197. University Books, New Hyde Park, New York.

31 Angus, S. (1966). *The Mystery Religions and Christianity*, 1st ed., pp. 196–197. New Hyde Park, New York: University Books.

32 Sheldon, H. 1918. *The Mystery Religions and the New Testament*, 1st ed., p. 24. New York, Cincinnati: The Abingdon Press.

33 Walsh, P. G. n.d. "Making a Drama out of a Crisis: Livy on the Bacchanalia." Greece and Rome 43 (2): 188–203. https://doi.org/10.1093/gr/43.2.188.

34 Case, Shirley, (1914) *Christanity and the Mystery Religions*, 1st ed., p. 8. The Biblical World.

35 Case, Shirley, (1914) *Christanity and the Mystery Religions*, 1st ed., p. 8. The Biblical World.

36 Case, Shirley, (1914) *Christanity and the Mystery Religions*, 1st ed., p. 8. The Biblical World.

37 MacArthur, John. "The Truth About Tongues Part 1 and 2." Sermon, Grace Community Church, June 9 and 16, 1977.

38 Reitzenstein, Richard. 1978. *Hellenistic Mystery-Religions: Their Basic Ideas and Significance*, pp. 42–43. Pittsburgh: Pickwick Press.

39 Riggs, James Stevenson and Reed, Larry Lathrop. 1922. *Epistle to the Corinthians: 1 Corinthians*, p. 113. New York: Macmillan Press.

About the Author

R. L. Pich has served in Christian ministry for over fifty years as a teacher, author, musician, and Sunday school facilitator. He holds an associate, two bachelor's, and two master's degrees in multiple fields of study, including a Bible degree from San Diego Christian College. He has been married for over fifty years and has three grown children, fourteen grandchildren, and two great-grandchild. His passion is to help others grow in the grace and knowledge of our Lord Jesus Christ.